THE ROAD TO BLUE

★ ★

A PHOTO ESSAY OF THE
OHIO DEMOCRATS' RETURN TO LEADERSHIP

THE ROAD TO BLUE

★ ★

A PHOTO ESSAY OF THE
OHIO DEMOCRATS' RETURN TO LEADERSHIP

Introduction by
John Glenn

Photography and Art Direction
Nannette Bedway

Contributing Photographers
Jamie Janos
Thom Sivo
Ryan DiVita

Design by
Kim Brown

Production by
Orbit Design, Inc.

Edited by
Suzanne Goldsmith Hirsch

Published by
Victory Publishing LLC
COLUMBUS

The Road to Blue: A Photo Essay of the Ohio Democrats' Return to Leadership

10 9 8 7 6 5 4 3 2 1

Published by Victory Publishing LLC
550 East Walnut Street
Columbus, Ohio 43215

Printed in Ohio.

To the many who have shared
Ohio's journey on the Road to Blue…

The stretch of Route 35 between Chillicothe and Jackson was completed as a result of the Southern Ohio Compact, negotiated by then U.S. Representative Ted Strickland with the Ohio Department of Transportation.

TABLE OF CONTENTS

INTRODUCTION

As far back as I can remember, I have believed in the importance of government as the most important chance we have to protect our right to "...liberty and justice for all." It was just over 200 years ago that the Constitution of the United States established just such a form of government for the first time.

Through the years, to make it work, political parties were formed that represented differing views of how this young nation should develop. While parties and policies have changed through the years, it is notable that our Democratic Party has remained as the longest continuously serving political body in history. In my heart, I believe it is because the Democratic Party, through all of its political ups and downs, has the best overall record of serving the interests of all the people of our nation.

It has been 16 years since the Democratic Party last held leadership at the statewide level. Now, the Ohio political situation has changed. It's a new time, with a new team, consisting of United States Senator Sherrod Brown, Governor Ted Strickland, Lt. Governor Lee Fisher, Attorney General Marc Dann, Secretary of State Jennifer Brunner, and Treasurer Rich Cordray.

Ohio has many opportunities for growth but it also has many challenges. I believe our new Democratic team brings a fresh vision for moving Ohio forward. I sense an unwavering determination and commitment to build on the rich heritage we have as leaders in the world. It is a vision that calls upon each of us to embrace our diversity and to work in harmony as we face the problems of an ever changing and complex world.

This book is a photo essay of the Democratic Party's return to statewide leadership. I hope it provides you an opportunity to become more familiar with each of the new team members. I believe you will be as proud to have them serve you as Annie and I are.

Best Regards,

John Glenn

John Glenn

◄ *Annie and John Glenn, Columbus 2007. The Glenns are photographed in front of a painting of Senator Glenn's childhood home, painted by John and Annie's daughter, Lyn Glenn.*

THE ROAD TO...

SHERROD ★ BROWN

When Sherrod Brown decided to give up his seat in the House of Representatives and run for the U.S. Senate, he laid some ground rules for the challenging year ahead:

He would run as a true progressive. No tip-toeing to the middle-of-the-road, becoming a "safer" candidate guided by fear, rather than principle. Sherrod was going to take to the voters his fight for the working men and women of Ohio because he knew that *his* progressive values were *their* values, too, on the issues that mattered most: jobs, healthcare, education and the war in Iraq.

◄ *Sherrod on the steps of the Ohio Statehouse in October 2007 (left); Sherrod discusses his campaign priorities for a better Ohio (above).*

Sherrod would run his campaign in all 88 counties of Ohio, which included some of the most conservative pockets in the Midwest. Many Republicans and Independents, not just Democrats, were unhappy with the direction of their country, and Sherrod would not concede a single vote to the status quo.

Sherrod and his wife Connie Schultz share a quiet moment on the campaign trail. Schultz, a Pulitzer Prize-winning columnist for the Cleveland Plain Dealer, *took a leave from her job to campaign full-time for Sherrod. While campaigning, Connie wrote a book, "...And his Lovely Wife," which chronicled life on the trail.* ▶

◀ Sherrod pledged to protect the jobs of working families as he traveled across the state.

Sherrod and Ted Strickland, longtime colleagues in the U.S. House of Representatives, pause for a quick snapshot. ▶

Sherrod was never too busy to stop and talk with supporters while on the campaign trail. ▼

▲ *Sherrod talks about the issues.*

Whenever his opponent attacked him, Sherrod would fight back—
and hard. Not with lies or ugly campaign ads, but with the truth.
No more lying down for vicious swift boat-like attacks that trafficked
in smear and innuendo.

Finally, Sherrod insisted on a coordinated campaign with his longtime friend, gubernatorial candidate Ted Strickland. Sherrod and Ted had served together in Congress, and together they would work hard to improve the lives of all Ohioans.

◄ *Sherrod listens to concerns of two constituents during a campaign stop.*

Sherrod, a Mansfield native, had held elected office in Ohio for more than 30 years by the time he ran for the U.S. Senate. His parents, Charles and Emily Brown, raised him to believe there was no higher calling than to serve others. They attended church regularly, and Sherrod and both his brothers were Eagle Scouts.

Throughout the race, Sherrod wore a pin depicting a canary in a cage, which soon became the symbol for his campaign. The canary represented the struggle for economic and social justice in our country.

"In the early days of the 20th century, more than 2000 American workers were killed in coal mines every year," Sherrod said, over and over. "Miners took a canary into the mines to warn them of toxic gases. If the canary died, they knew they had to escape quickly. Miners were forced to provide for their own protection. There were no mine safety laws, no trade unions able to help. And no real support from their government."

▲ *Ohio's Junior Senator with Ohio's legendary Senator, John Glenn, and Connie at an event celebrating Governor Ted Strickland's Inauguration.*

Sherrod's canary pin was a reminder of the progressives' 100-year battle to improve the lives of all Americans. Their efforts led to clean air and safe drinking water, auto safety rules, Medicare and Medicaid, Social Security, civil rights laws, protections for the disabled and prohibitions on child labor.

▲ *Sherrod gives some of the points of his plan for a better Ohio.*

"Remarkably, it was ordinary working families who won so many of these battles against the most entrenched, well-heeled interests."

— Sherrod Brown

▲ *Sherrod smiles after being sworn in.*

◄ *Sherrod stops to talk with a throng of supporters.*

Sherrod, Connie and family watch election returns and wait for the good news in their hotel room in Cleveland. ▶

Sherrod and Connie wait for the final counts. ▼

That battle, he insisted, was far from over.

The overwhelming majority of Ohio voters agreed. In the end, Sherrod won by more than 12 points.

On election night, he assured the standing-room-only crowd of supporters that Sherrod Brown was not the only winner:

"Today, in Ohio, in the middle of America, the middle class won."

Sherrod with Connie and his mother, Emily Brown (below, left); Sherrod with good friend Dennis Eckhart (below, right). ▼

▲ Sherrod is sworn in by Governor Ted Strickland.

◄ Shaking hands and thanking supporters, Sherrod moves through the crowd on election night.

SECRETARY OF STATE
JENNIFER ★ BRUNNER

Jennifer Brunner's commitment to public service comes naturally—
it's genetic. Her political pedigree stretches back 19 generations to
her ancestors Digery Priest, an original signer of the Mayflower
Compact, and her uncle Marcus Hanna, the campaign chair for
President William McKinley.

The seeds for Jennifer's 2006 run were sown in 1983 when she went to work for then Secretary
of State Sherrod Brown. She loved the work. She was a natural with the intricacies of
election law. And her passion for the office was cemented early with an awareness of the
enormous responsibility it has for upholding our democracy.

◄ *Jennifer Brunner, October 2007 (left); Jennifer gives her victory speech to a standing room only crowd
on election night (above).*

★ ★

Jennifer's prior service as Legislative Counsel for the Secretary of State's Office, 13 years of election law private practice experience, including serving as a special prosecutor for election fraud, and past experience as a member of the Franklin County Board of Elections clearly prepared her to be an effective and fair secretary of state.

★ ★

▲ Jennifer gives a speech at the last stop of her announcement tour.

Jennifer visits with Kay Giardini in Lorain County. ▼

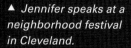

▲ Jennifer speaks at a neighborhood festival in Cleveland.

▲ *Jennifer's mother and stepfather, Barbara and John Gates, listen as Jennifer gives her inaugural address.*

◄ *Ted and Fran Alberty, longtime Democratic activist and supporter, and Jennifer are photographed at the Franklin County Democratic Party Dinner.*

Politics is all about timing. And for Jennifer Brunner, the right time came in 2004 during her fourth year serving as a judge in the Franklin County Court of Common Pleas. Aware that the current secretary of state was term-limited, she decided to pursue her long standing dream to run for the office in 2006.

Jennifer takes a break to share a photo with Sophie Schoolcraft while attending the Jefferson County Fall Dinner in Mingo Junction. ►

Jennifer, Jan Roller, U.S. Representative Stephanie Tubbs Jones and Peggy Wilkinson at a campaign event in Cleveland. ►

"To improve the lives of everyday Ohioans we serve, we must identify and index those factors necessary to help them reach their full potential. As the keeper of Ohio's records, the secretary of state is in the best position to do this work."

— Jennifer Brunner

▲ Brunner campaign field coordinator Kellye Pinkelton hands out Brunner stickers with the Democrat mascot at the Geauga County Fair.

Friends on the trail...Frances Strickland and Jennifer are photographed together at one of their many joint appearances during 2006. ▶

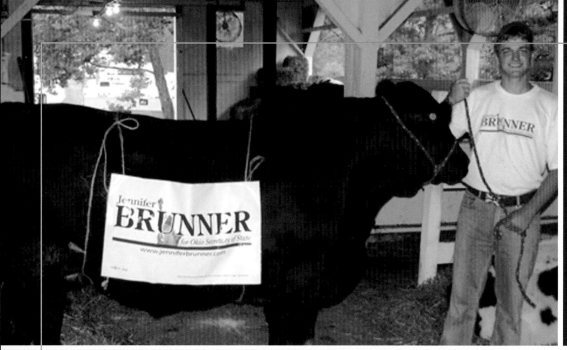

◄ A well-placed sign... Ben Hobbs shows a steer at the Columbiana County Fair.

To make the run, Jennifer made the tough choice to step away from a seat on the bench where every day she had the opportunity to have a personal impact on many lives. As she crisscrossed Ohio in her campaign's Chevy Suburban, affectionately referred to as the "War Wagon," Jennifer became increasingly aware that her pledge to conduct free, fair and accountable elections had tapped into a hunger across the Ohio landscape. By the end of the campaign, and after thousands of miles traveled and cities and citizens visited, Jennifer realized that the unique thread that connected it all was the need for leadership.

▲ Jennifer talks about her plan with Ohioans.

◄ Jennifer is joined by Lieutenant Governor candidate Lee Fisher during her announcement tour in Toledo.

30

The campaign brought with it the shared joys of family. Rick, AKA "Mr. Jennifer Brunner," was the driver, Man Friday, and all around campaign support system. One of the Brunners' daughters, Kate, left her job with the Ohio Supreme Court to come on board, and their son John postponed a semester of college to become Jennifer's aide/driver. Their daughter Laura traveled in from Boston frequently to lend a hand. Jennifer's mother moved back to Ohio from Louisiana to speak on Jennifer's behalf in scores of Ohio's 88 counties. Even the family dogs were War Wagon passengers on the trail.

▲ *Rick Brunner, Jennifer's husband, driver, and campaign speaker drives to yet another campaign stop in Gallipolis during the southeastern Ohio leg of the announcement tour (above, left); supporter Andrea Dowding welcomes Jennifer to Dresden in Muskingum County (above, right).*

A campaign's best friends…Jake and Max in the War Wagon. ▶

▲ Secretary of State-Elect Brunner is joined on the stage on election night by Ohio House Minority Leader, Representative Joyce Beatty; State Treasurer-Elect Richard Cordray; and State Representative Tracy Heard.

Amazing family and friends, amazing volunteers and amazing staff— they made it all possible. On November 7, 2006, Jennifer Brunner was elected Ohio Secretary of State.

◄ Rick and daughters Kate and Laura listen as Jennifer gives her inaugural speech.

Daughter Laura Brunner sings with members of a jazz band at the inaugural celebration (below, left); Jennifer's mom, Barbara Gates, son John, and niece Mollie Dowding (below, right). ▼

"Free and fair elections in Ohio. Never again will that be forgotten in our great state." – Jennifer Brunner

▲ Jennifer is sworn in at her inauguration by Montgomery County Common Pleas Judge A.J. Wagner with husband Rick holding the Bible she studied while in college at Miami University.

Jennifer signs an autograph at an inaugural event. ▶

33

THE ROAD TO ...

STATE TREASURER
RICHARD ★ CORDRAY

As 2005 melted into 2006, Rich Cordray's campaign for State Treasurer appeared to be an uphill climb. Rich had been on the statewide ticket in 1998 and he anticipated a tough campaign against a slate of well-known, experienced candidates.

The would-be treasurer from Grove City, Ohio was no stranger to a challenge. Rich entered the race with a degree from Michigan State University, a master's in economics from Oxford University and a law degree from the University of Chicago Law School. Rich was also a five-time champion on the television game show *Jeopardy*. Rich Cordray embraces competition.

◀ *State Treasurer Richard Cordray, October 2007; Rich visits with Ohioans on a beautiful summer day during the campaign (above).*

By early 2006, Rich had a strong team working on his campaign, bringing together some seasoned pros and a growing group of young people, enthusiastic about the prospect for change in Ohio.

"We worked on making the case for a new direction for the state and especially how the government handles Ohio's finances. We found that these themes resonated with voters."

— Richard Cordray

▲ At a campaign stop, Rich chats with supporters.

In places like Washington Courthouse, Columbus and Cleveland, Rich campaigned on a platform of integrity and sensible fiscal leadership.

Rich stops for a snapshot with Dayton Mayor, Rhine McLin. ▶

With open ears
and an open
mind, Rich went
directly to the
people.

Rich asked about their concerns—about their worries. And he asked them how he could help.

Over and over, people spoke to him about Ohio's bright past and their hopes for a brighter future.

Their words reminded Rich of the song, "Danny Boy." Right now, he thought, summer is in the

meadow—and if ever there was time for a rebirth in Ohio, that time was now.

Rich shares a laugh with then Ohio Senate Minority Leader, C.J. Prentiss. ▶

◀ Special Day... Rich with U.S. Representative, John Lewis.

Lorain County Commissioner Betty Blair walks with Rich in a parade. ▼

★ ★

Rich drew upon the legacy of his mentor, Mary Ellen Withrow, former Ohio and United States Treasurer. Rich pledged to restore the Withrow emphasis on small business assistance. It was Mary Ellen, too, who advised him to emphasize his years as a county treasurer and how that experience would help him solve Ohio's economic issues.

★ ★

▼ *The would-be state treasurer is pictured here with his mentor, former U.S. Treasurer, Mary Ellen Withrow at the Marion Popcorn Festival.*

Rich, his wife Peggy, a Capital Law School professor, and their two children, Holly and Danny, were frequently together for parades and campaign stops, like a visit to the Henry County Radish Festival.

▲ Rich partakes of the signature vegetable at the McClure Radish Festival in Henry County (above, left); Rich speaks with a supporter about some points of his plan (above, right).

Lee, Rich and Ted share some camaraderie on the campaign trail. ▶

"Being part of the Turnaround Ohio Tours was the highlight of the campaign. On our first weekend, we addressed large enthusiastic crowds in at least 16 counties. I could tell there was something in the air—I could tell we were onto something really great."

— Richard Cordray

A tireless campaigner, Rich talks with supporters while on the campaign trail. ▼

▲ *Rich gives a speech outlining his strategy to get Ohio back on track.*

▲ Peggy holds Rich's Bible as he is sworn in by Mary Ellen Withrow.

◄ Peggy and the Cordray twins, Holly and Danny, at Rich's inauguration.

THE ROAD TO...

ATTORNEY GENERAL
MARC ★ DANN

In the fall of 2006, it often seemed as if there were only two people who thought Marc Dann was going to be elected: the candidate and his driver.

The candidate, however, was experienced. Marc Dann's career in public service includes posts as a state senator, attorney and Liberty Local School District school board member. Marc, a Cleveland native, holds degrees from the University of Michigan and Case Western Reserve University.

And the driver was not just any driver. It was his daughter Mia—and she was committed to helping her father win.

◄ *Attorney General Marc Dann, October 2007 (left); Marc addresses a standing room only crowd during a campaign stop during 2006 (above).*

Mia spent countless hours with her father on the road, keeping him prepped and ready for his next event. Some of Marc's happiest times on the campaign trail were the long stretches between cities when he and Mia could have conversations on just about everything.

One of Mia's jobs was to keep her father away from fast food. She had her hands full, especially when it came to keeping an eye on him at county fairs!

▲ Fellow candidates Barbara Sykes and Jennifer Brunner walk with the crowds assembled for a rally in Cleveland in the fall of 2006 (above, left); another fellow candidate, Zack Space, campaigns at a backyard barbecue in Zanesville during his successful bid for U.S. Representative in the 18th District (above, right).

Hundreds of supporters gather in Cleveland for a rally. ▶

▲ *Marc is pictured here with his wife, Alyssa Lenhoff, (above, left); the Dann Children: Jessie, Mia and Charlie (above, right).*

Otis, the Dann family dog, was no stranger to the campaign trail. ▶

In fact, the entire Dann family often spent their weekends campaigning. Marc's wife Alyssa, an investigative reporter by trade, and their three children, Mia, Charlie, and Jessie, were frequent visitors to county events around the state during the course of the campaign. Even Otis, the family dog, was not spared campaign duty. Each day on the campaign trail brought incredible lessons and fun for the entire Dann family.

A familiar sight to Marc Dann during his time in the legislature, the atrium is energized with activity in anticipation of inaugural activitities. ▶

Marc's campaign was driven by one motivating factor: to make state government work better for the citizens of Ohio.

Many of the principles that guided Marc's attorney general campaign reflected his good work while in the Ohio Senate. As a senator, Marc worked tirelessly as an advocate for our troops, fighting for additional body armor funding. He fought to protect our environment by introducing legislation to place a moratorium on new construction debris landfills. And everyday, he worked on behalf of our families, children and seniors, on a range of critical issues including healthcare and Social Security.

▼ Marc's dedicated campaign staff takes a moment to pose for a photo with Marc's son, Charlie (kneeling).

◄ U.S. Representative Marcy Kaptur, 9th District, and volunteers campaign for Marc Dann, Ted Strickland, Lee Fisher and the statewide ticket in the Toledo area.

Marc talks about healthcare and protecting our seniors with two supporters. ▶

Marc and two supporters at the Ashville Fair. ▶

◄ Jessie and some friends campaign for her dad.

A campaign volunteer introduces Marc to another Ohioan concerned about the future of our state. ▶

54

◄ Marc pauses from his frenzied campaign schedule to pose for a photo with two supporters at a festival in Columbus.

Marc was often joined by Charlie on the campaign trail. Here, Charlie and Marc are seen at the 2006 Ohio Democratic Party State Dinner, which was attended by almost 3,000 party faithful. ▶

Marc offers remarks at a campaign event. ▼

▲ A collective spirit of positive change was felt by the hundreds of attendees at Marc's inauguration.

◀ Marc is greeted by Carol Pennington, an avid supporter, at a campaign stop in northwest Ohio.

Months after the campaign, Marc offered a summary of what it all meant to him:

"The election of 2006 is the story of strong hands that came together to grab hold of big dreams. Those dreams guide me."

— Marc Dann

▲ Marc is sworn in as Attorney General by Judge Bill O'Neill. He is joined at the podium by Alyssa.

◀ With his family by his side, Marc thanks supporters.

LIEUTENANT GOVERNOR
LEE ★ FISHER

In early 2005, shortly before U.S. Representative Ted Strickland announced his candidacy for governor, Lee Fisher and Ted enjoyed a long breakfast at a Bob Evans in Rootstown, Ohio. They talked about family, life, politics, and their common vision for Ohio.

Having served as state representative, state senator, attorney general, statewide chair of the 1992 Clinton-Gore campaign, and the 1998 Democratic nominee for governor, Lee understood the pivotal importance of the 2006 election to the future of the state, and to the nation.

◄ Lieutenant Governor Lee Fisher, October 2007 (left); Lee and Ted talk about their Turnaround Ohio Plan (above).

Throughout 2005, Ted and Lee continued to talk, and in January 2006, Ted asked Lee to join him on the ticket as candidate for lieutenant governor and a special, successful partnership was formed. Asked by the media if he could adjust to his new role, Lee noted that this was nothing new for him— he had been lieutenant governor of the Fisher family household for the past 26 years.

▼ *The Fisher Family... Lee, Peggy, Jason, Jessica, and dog Sam.*

*New leadership...
Ted Strickland and
Lee Fisher.* ▶

◀ *Lee and Peggy share a
happy moment with friends
on the campaign trail.*

*Ted and Lee talk
about the future.* ▶

The lives of the Fisher family members changed in an instant. On the same day that Lee made the tough choice to give up his seven-year position as president and CEO of the Center for Families and Children in order to campaign with Ted full-time, Peggy took a new full-time job as president and CEO of the Diversity Center of Northeast Ohio. At the same time, their daughter Jessica enrolled in a new high school and their son Jason graduated from college. Jason moved back home to film a documentary about the governor's race.

▲ Peggy and Jessica share a hug (above, left); Lee with Representative Joyce Beatty, minority leader in the Ohio House, and Senator Teresa Fedor, minority leader in the Ohio Senate (above, right).

Lee's father Stan, and brother, Richard, join him for an inaugural reception. ▶

◀ Jason helps his father with his lapel microphone just prior to the ecumenical prayer service held at Trinity Episcopal Church in Columbus on the day of Ted and Lee's public swearing-in ceremony. Jason chronicled the campaign in a documentary film, "Swing State."

Peggy generously allowed the entire first floor of the Fisher home to be converted into a 24/7 campaign office. Lee described it as a "friendly takeover." Despite occasional interruptions by Sam, the family dog, Lee and his talented, dedicated team of Laura Fleming, Tazeem Pasha, and Erin White, along with a team of loyal volunteers, operated directly from the Fisher kitchen table—adding a whole new meaning to the term "kitchen cabinet."

◀ Lee and Peggy with their hardworking campaign staff (from left) Tazeem Pasha, Laura Fleming and Erin White.

Jason and John tape footage for their campaign documentary, "Swing State." ▶

Lee poses with Betty Sutton, newly elected U.S. Representative from Ohio's 13th District. ▼

In addition to his daily fundraising, Lee campaigned throughout the state, often joined by Jason and his college friend and film partner, John Intrater. On weekends, Peggy and Jessica joined Lee and Jason on the campaign trail in the Fisher family Buick.

One of Lee's favorite moments on the campaign trail was singing with Frances at the Belmont County Democratic Party dinner, to the tune of "Davy Crockett."

Some of the lyrics included...

"My wife Peggy answered the phone one evening late; it was Ted asking me to be his running mate; As happy as I was, one thing is clear; if he had heard me sing, I doubt I'd be here!"

Peggy fields one of the daily deluge of campaign calls for the team (below, left); Jason and Lee campaign for the Strickland-Fisher ticket (below, right). ▼

▼ *Lee and Frances perform a reprise of their campaign song at the Breakfast with Friends event.*

"We have a responsibility not only to do more with less, but also to do more for those who have less. And we have an opportunity to do that if we lift and grow our economy, because a rising tide lifts all boats."

— Lee Fisher

Lee especially enjoyed traveling on the campaign bus with Ted and the entire statewide ticket and the countless opportunities to introduce Ted at campaign events. Lee joked that he introduced Ted so often that he felt like he, too, had grown up on Duck Run.

Lee talks about the Turnaround Ohio Plan. ▶

▲ Lee poses with State Representative Barbara Boyd and her daughter, Janine Boyd, at the Dinner with Friends, an inaugural celebration event.

At the public ceremony, Lee was sworn in by his father, Stan, on Torahs belonging to his children and late mother, and on Peggy's Bible. As Stan recited the oath of office a little too quickly, Lee laughed and asked his father to slow down—a funny moment in an otherwise serious and historic ceremony. This was an event that launched the beginning of a new Ohio governor and lieutenant governor, a new administration, and a new team of statewide office holders who would turn around Ohio.

◄ Lee greets supporters on election night at the Hyatt on Capitol Square in Columbus.

▲ Ohio Supreme Court Justice Thomas Moyer swears in Lee during a private ceremony in the governor's statehouse office at midnight on January 8, 2007. The public ceremony followed on Saturday, January 13, on the statehouse west lawn.

◄ After thousands of miles traveled, countless events, and non-stop campaigning all across Ohio, Ted and Lee celebrate victory together on election night.

THE ROAD TO ...

TED ★ STRICKLAND

Perhaps the most quoted statement of Ted Strickland's campaign for Governor came from his description of his family's living quarters after a fire took their home on Duck Run when he was only four years old. "Believe me; if you learn anything from living in a chicken shack, it's that things can get better."

That optimism in the face of adversity is one of Ted's most important guiding principles. It's what led him to run for governor: Ted knew things could be better in Ohio. As a Methodist minister, a children's home director and a 12 year member of the U.S. House of Representatives from Ohio's 6th District, Ted has always worked to improve the lives of everyday Ohioans. Roger Strickland, Ted's brother, says it's in his nature. "I think Ted wakes up every day thinking, 'What can I do to help someone?'"

◀ *Governor Ted Strickland, October 2007 (left); Ted greets supporters and shakes hands with Clover Elliott at a Cleveland rally in October 2006 (above).*

▼ *Frances Strickland, October 2007.*

Frances, Ted's wife of almost 20 years, brought her own boundless energy and fun spirit to the campaign trail. Traveling almost as much as her candidate husband, Frances was seen brandishing her guitar and singing Ted's bio song to the tune of "Davy Crockett" at countless county Democratic Party dinners and campaign stops. Frances spearheaded the organization of the Strickland Singers, a campaign choir, with members from all over Ohio, who sang at Ted's rallies and inspired large crowds. A great lover of music, Frances also helped to compile a campaign CD of songs written and performed by Ohio artists supporting the positive message of Ted and the rest of the Democratic statewide slate. "I knew that campaigns with music were successful—I wanted to bring that spirit of fun to our efforts in Ohio," Frances says.

Sharing Ted's deep desire to turn around Ohio, Frances spoke on the campaign trail about many issues, especially the need to make improvements in education. Today, as First Lady, Frances continues to travel around the state acting as a positive change agent for education, inclusion and the environment.

Frances' parents, Anna Belle and George Frank Smith attend the inaugural event, Breakfast with Friends. ▶

Family ties... Ted spends some time with his siblings, nieces and nephews. ▼

▲ *Frances surprised Ted by performing his bio song at the 2006 Ohio Democratic Party state dinner. Picking out the chords herself on an acoustic guitar, Frances sang while Ted gave his own running (and funny) commentary. It was an instant hit, and one she was often called upon to repeat along the campaign trail. Even the video was a sensation, generating thousands of hits on YouTube.*

◀ *Members of the campaign choir, the Strickland Singers, directed by Joyce Robinson and Debbie Parker, perform at a rally in Cleveland.*

Ted has always been a tireless campaigner, and in his run for governor, he was no different. On the campaign trail, Ted and the other statewide candidates formed a close relationship and gave each other energy. Ted also had the benefit of Frances who campaigned for him full-time.

Ted thanks a supporter (right); Frances marches in one of many parades during Ted's campaign for governor (below, left); Roger Strickland and campaign staffer Elizabeth Scott photographed at Ted's annual birthday party held at the Scioto County Fairgrounds in Lucasville (below, right). ▼

Guests gather backstage after the Cleveland debate. Debates were also held in Columbus, Cincinnati and Youngstown. ▶

▲ (Clockwise, from top) Ted and Frances at a picnic in northeast Ohio; equally committed to the environment and conservation, Ted and Frances fish with some friends; Ted signs the first of many bumper stickers at a campaign event.

Lou Gentile, Ted's aide, traveled with him the most and covered thousands of miles with the candidate. One night, after countless hours on the road and non-stop events, Lou was heard saying about Ted, "He never gets tired. The man isn't human."

Ted knew that voters were weary of divisiveness in political campaigns, and he was determined not to run a negative campaign. His commitment to friends and supporters was to run strictly on the issues. He wanted Ohioans to unite behind a common vision of how things could be. It was a message that worked.

▲ Shop talk... Ted meets with his running mate, Lee Fisher, and staffer Janetta King on his Turnaround Ohio initiatives.

"There is nothing wrong with our state that can't be fixed with our hard work, our passion, and our creativity."

— Ted Strickland

▲ Ted talks with farmers about Ohio's agricultural industry and its economic importance for the state (above, left); Roger Strickland, Ted's brother, traveled in the Sportsmen for Strickland RV, adding his own unique sense of humor and fun to the campaign trail (above, right); Ted and his friend, U.S. Representative Tim Ryan, share a fun moment on the campaign trail (middle).

"If we trust our future to the hopes and dreams of the average Ohioan, the dividend we'll see will be the return of Ohio's greatness."

— Governor's Inaugural Address

Statewide candidates, Ben Espy, Barbara Sykes, Marc Dann, Richard Cordray, and Columbus Mayor Michael B. Coleman are joined by members of the Ohio Legislative Black Caucus at the 2006 Ohio Democratic Party State Dinner in Columbus (below, left); Ted thanks a supporter, Lisel Sondheimer (below, right). ▼

▲ Ohio's First Brother, Roger Strickland, joins Frances on stage the night of Ted's election victory. Also on the stage, Frances and Roger are joined by, from left, John Corrigan, Abigail Corrigan, Tim Corrigan and Angela Dombrowski, long-time personal friends of the Stricklands.

Ted and Frances are honored and humbled by the awesome responsibility of taking Ohio down a new road.

▼ Ted and campaign manager, John Haseley, are photographed in the Governor's office shortly after the private swearing-in ceremony. John, Ted's long-time Congressional chief-of-staff, returned from Washington, D.C., to manage Ted's campaign.

◄ Ted signs his first executive order as governor. The document, aimed at strictly limiting meals and gifts, is a promise to the people of Ohio that he and his staff will abide by the highest ethical standards during their time in office.

▲ Ted is sworn-in by Chief Justice Thomas Moyer at a private ceremony held in the Governor's Statehouse office at midnight on January 8, 2007. Ted is joined by his brother, Roger, three of his sisters, Jean, Shirley and Helen, his brother-in-law, Mike, and Frances.

◄ Jessica Fisher holds a paper chain created during the campaign by volunteer Angela Bachman. On the links were the names and counties of volunteers who gave their time and energy to help turn around Ohio. Over 50 feet long, the chain snaked its way through the crowded hotel ballroom on election night, eventually ending in the hands of the new governor and first lady.

81

THE ROAD TO...

State Representative Chris Redfern served as the chairman of the Ohio Democratic Party during the 2006 election cycle. Chris rebuilt the Party from the grassroots, garnering support and excitement from Democrats in all 88 counties. The prominence of the Democratic Party and the importance of the statewide elections, began to attract national attention, and the Democratic National Committee worked extensively with the state Party to invest time and resources into securing victories in November. Chris's commitment to Ohio and the Party trickled down to Ohioans ready for a change and showed the nation that Ohio was about to embark on a major turnaround.

Chris and Ohio Democratic Party staffer Lakshmi Satyanarayana campaign for Ted and Lee (right); Chris and then State Senator Charlie Wilson, who won a decisive victory in his 6th district bid for the U.S. House of Representatives are photographed at the Dinner with Friends (far right). ▶

Kim and Chris Redfern are joined by Donna and Bill Hartnett at the Dinner with Friends on inauguration weekend. ▼

▲ Chris delivers one of his energetic speeches to motivate supporters at a campaign event.

◀ Chris talks with members of the Ohio Democratic Party Women's Caucus.

85

The importance of the Ohio elections did not go unnoticed by the rest of the country. Friends from all over the United States traveled to the Buckeye state to help in the effort to turn around Ohio. Speaking at rallies, county Democratic Party dinners, fundraisers and other events, out-of-town visitors—led, most notably, by President Bill Clinton—helped to deliver the excitement necessary to energize volunteers, supporters and voters. Ohio was once again the center of national and even international press attention as a political bellwether for the nation.

◄ Led by Ohio Democatic Party Chairman, Chris Redfern, national leaders, activists, volunteers and supporters came together in the perfect storm to turn around Ohio.

▲ Former U.S. Senators Max Cleland and John Edwards, U.S. Senators Joseph Biden, Hillary Rodham Clinton and Barack Obama, and U.S. Representatives Dennis Kucinich and Jay Inslee were frequently seen on the 2006 campaign trail in Ohio.

THE ROAD TO ...

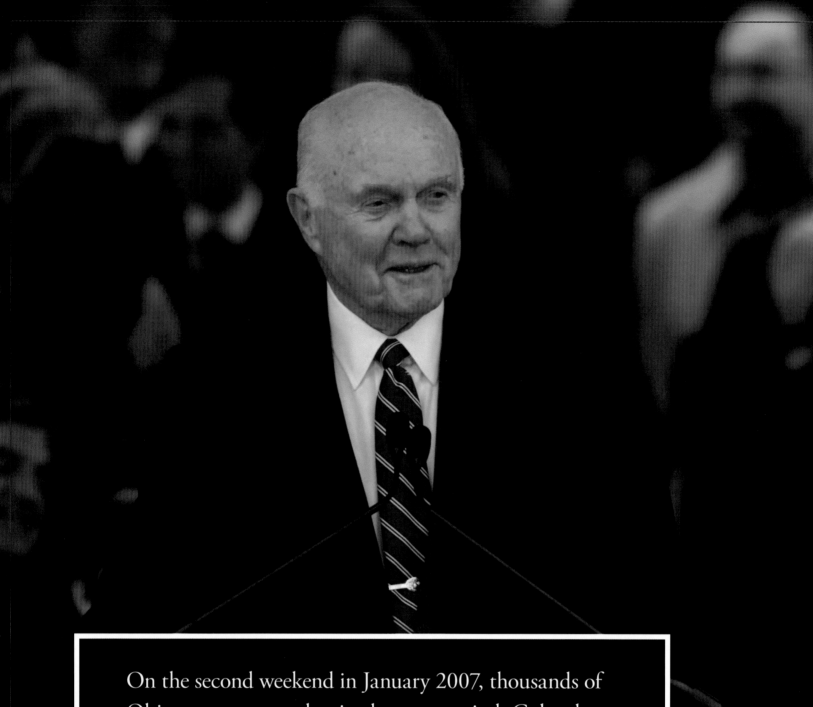

On the second weekend in January 2007, thousands of Ohioans came together in the state capital, Columbus, to celebrate the inauguration of Ted Strickland and Lee Fisher and the other newly-elected Democratic statewide officeholders. Inaugural Committee Co-Chairs Annie and John Glenn, and Committee President David J. Leland oversaw the massive planning and organization of the weekend.

The purpose of the inaugural events was clear — to unite and show appreciation for the Ohioans who had devoted countless hours and effort toward campaigning for the Democratic ticket in 2006. Campaign volunteers, public officials and supporters, along with the friends and family members of the newly elected officials, came together on the inaugural weekend to celebrate a new beginning in Ohio.

The festivities kicked off Friday night with a "Dinner with Friends" at the Statehouse, where Ted and Lee expressed their deep appreciation to public officials for their hard work during the campaign. The next morning, an ecumenical prayer service at Trinity Episcopal Church began a full day of events. Inaugural guests were treated to an Inaugural Tribute to Dr. Martin Luther King, Jr., in celebration of his holiday weekend, and a celebration of the arts at "Beautiful Ohio: A Public Celebration."

The public oath of office ceremony for Ted and Lee took place on the West Lawn of the Ohio Statehouse at 11:30 a.m. Under a light drizzle, more than 1,000 guests watched as Ohio's new governor and lieutenant governor were sworn into office. Following the ceremony, Ted and Frances, along with Lee and Peggy, greeted the public in the atrium of the Statehouse.

Saturday's events culminated with the Ohio Inaugural Ball, held in the Lausche and Rhodes Buildings at the Ohio State Fairgrounds. Over 5,000 friends old and new came together to dance and celebrate the historic new beginning at a festive black tie affair that featured the best of Ohio music and food.

◄ *Senator John Glenn, January 13, 2007 (left); Governor Ted Strickland delivers his inaugural address to an enthusiastic crowd on the West Lawn of the Ohio Statehouse (above).*

▲ Ted is joined by former Cincinnati Mayor Charlie Luken, Columbus Mayor Michael B. Coleman, and State Representative Kenny Yuko at the inaugural celebration event, Dinner with Friends, which was held in the Ohio Statehouse Atrium the night before the Strickland-Fisher public swearing-in ceremony.

◄ Then State Representative John Boccieri and Senator Glenn photographed at the Dinner with Friends.

Ted reaches to hug Annie Glenn as he welcomes her to the Dinner with Friends. ▼

▲ *A light rain could not dampen the spirits of a capacity crowd at the public swearing-in ceremony.*

▲ *The Ohio Statehouse Atrium alive with activity on inauguration day.*

▲ Ted and State Representative Fred Strahorn.

◀ Ted visits with State Representative Robert Hagan and his wife Michele.

Ted and Chris Cupples, the governor's personal assistant, travel to the service. ▶

Ted and Frances attend the morning ecumenical service at Trinity Episcopal Church in Columbus prior to the public swearing-in ceremony. Washington County residents and longtime supporters, Betty and Bob Boersma are seated across the aisle. ▼

Frances and Peggy take the stage at the Breakfast with Friends to thank supporters. ▶

▼ *Trinity Episcopal Church.*

Lee asked his Rabbi, Eric Bram, from Suburban Temple in Cleveland, to speak at the ecumenical service. ▶

▲ *Ted thanks the many guests who attended the performances of "Beautiful Ohio: A Public Celebration" at the Palace Theatre.*

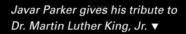

Javar Parker gives his tribute to Dr. Martin Luther King, Jr. ▼

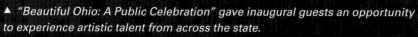
▲ "Beautiful Ohio: A Public Celebration" gave inaugural guests an opportunity to experience artistic talent from across the state.

▲ "Beautiful Ohio" participants: the Dublin Taiko Drummers, the Cleveland School of the Arts, the School for the Creative and Performing Arts in Cincinnati, the Bucket Boyz, the Zanesville High School Devilettes, Steve Free, Jessica Grove, Dwight Lenox and the Lenox Avenue Express, Ladies of Longford, Red {an Orchestra}, Spencer Myer, and Indira Satyapriva and the Nalanda School of Asian Indian Dance.

▲ Sherrod shows Ted a newspaper article about the day's events.

◄ Frances spots a familiar face in the crowd.

▲ Stan Fisher administers the oath of office for son Lee.

◄ Lee embraces daughter Jessica after he completes his oath of office.

▲ *Ohio Supreme Court Chief Justice Thomas Moyer swears in Ted as Ohio's 68th governor.*

▲ Ted and Frances are escorted to the West Lawn of the Ohio Statehouse before the ceremony.

Ted thanks Sergeant First Class Robert A. Scott for his performance of the National Anthem. ▶

◄ Trevor Henderson, a senior at Beechcroft High School in Columbus at the time, closes the inaugural ceremony with the song "What a Wonderful World," by Louis Armstrong.

Faith Esham performs the song "Simple Gifts" at the public swearing-in ceremony. ▶

▲ Lee with friend and philanthropist, Julia Fishelson (above, left); Frances laughs with inaugural guests (above, right).

◄ Ted and Sherrod pose with Ohio House Minority Leader Joyce Beatty and Ohio Senate Minority Leader Teresa Fedor.

The Lausche Building at the Ohio State Fairgrounds was transformed into brilliant blue for the ball. ▶

▼ *Ted and Frances share a first dance at the Ohio Inaugural Ball.*

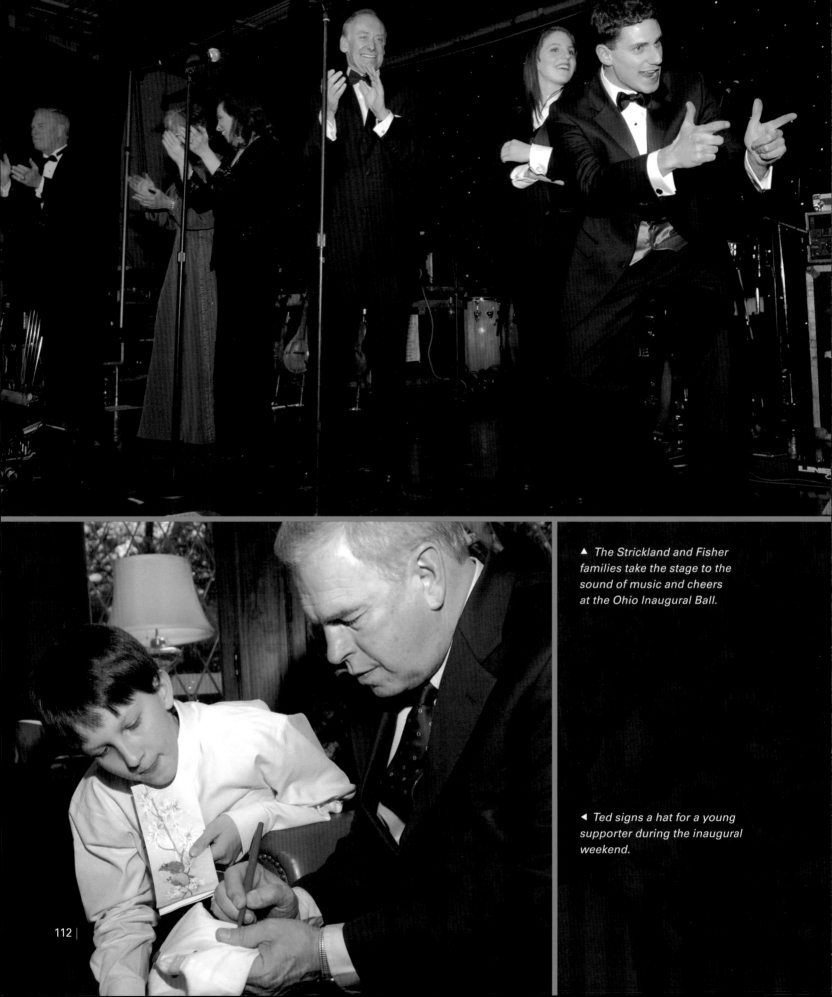

▲ The Strickland and Fisher families take the stage to the sound of music and cheers at the Ohio Inaugural Ball.

◄ Ted signs a hat for a young supporter during the inaugural weekend.

▲ Ted greets supporters who came to Columbus from across the state.

"At this very moment,
across the fields of our farms,
quietly echoing through the
canyons of our cityscapes,
and winding through a
thousand Ohio Main Streets
is the echo of hope."

— Ted Strickland

ACKNOWLEDGEMENTS

The publishers wish to thank the following individuals, who, without their help, this project would not have been possible.

Thank you...

Annie and John Glenn

Connie Schultz and Sherrod Brown
Jennifer and Rick Brunner
Peggy and Richard Cordray
Alyssa Lenhoff and Marc Dann
Peggy and Lee Fisher
Frances and Ted Strickland
Kim and Chris Redfern

Lisa Abraham
Kirsten Bedway
Kris Harrison and Gina Cronley of Orbit Design
Suzanne Goldsmith Hirsch
Elizabeth Maguire
Don McTigue
Juli Rogers of r design & printing
Jane Taylor
Mary Jane Veno
Degee and David Wilhelm
Antoinette and Mark Wilson

...to all of the many volunteers, supporters, friends and photographers of the campaigns of 2006, many of whom are in the photos of this book—thank you—for your help, your friendship, and your commitment to make Ohio a better place.